10 Reasons to Delete Social Media

Navigating the Digital World for a Healthier, Happier Life

By Isabella Hawthorne

"Social media is a tool, not a master. Reclaim your time, your attention, and your authentic self." - Unknown

Copyright © 2023

Table of Contents

Dedication

To all those who dare to disconnect and embrace the richness of life beyond the screen. May this book be a guide on your journey to a more mindful, meaningful existence.

—Isabella

Introduction: The Double-Edged Sword of Social Media

Welcome, dear reader, to the digital odyssey of our time, where every scroll, like, and share is a step into a world woven from pixels and predictions, likes and live streams. We stand on the precipice of a paradox—the grand enigma of social media. It's a universe within our universe, a place that can feel as close as the smartphone in our pocket and as vast as the cosmos.

Once upon a less digital time, the idea of instantly connecting with someone across the globe was the stuff of science fiction. Today, it's so commonplace that we don't even blink at the magic of it. Social media has become the town square, the family reunion, the classroom, and the protest march all rolled into one. It has the power to unite long-lost friends, ignite social movements, and provide a platform for voices that might otherwise go unheard.

Yet, for all its glittering promise, there's a shadow that trails behind the bright screen. In this bustling digital town square, we find ourselves speaking in echo chambers, hearing only the reverberations of our own voices and those like them. While we're more connected than ever, loneliness whispers in the corners of crowded digital rooms. We gather 'friends' like collectibles, yet the depth of those connections can be as fleeting as the stories that vanish after twenty-four hours.

And oh, how it entertains us! Our thumbs tirelessly wade through a never-ending stream of content—cat videos, memes, the latest dance craze, and snippets of life from people we admire (or envy). But this boundless entertainment comes at a price, measured in hours and minutes. It's a grand distraction, one that can turn minutes into hours, dinner tables silent, and the once vibrant art of conversation into a series of emoji exchanges.

This book isn't a manifesto to banish social media from the kingdom of technology. Nor is it a decree to declare it the villain in our modern narrative. Instead, it's an invitation to a grand exploration, a safari through the wilds of likes and follows, to discover the beast that is social media in all its glory and its cunning.

As we embark on this journey together, we'll delve into the caverns of comparison and climb the mountains of misinformation. We'll meet the specters of privacy invasion and confront the trolls under the bridges of online discourse. We'll wrestle with the paradox of connection and isolation, laughter and frustration, reality and illusion.

So, take my virtual hand, brave explorer. Let us embark on this adventure with open minds and ready hearts. May we navigate the labyrinth of social media with humor, insight, and the occasional cat meme to light our way. After all, if we can't share a laugh about our modern conundrums, are we truly as connected as we think?

Onward we go, to uncover the ten reasons you might just want to hit that 'log out' button, for a little while or perhaps for good.

Chapter 1: The Comparison Carousel

Step right up, step right up! Welcome to the dazzling, dizzying Comparison Carousel – social media's most enchanting ride. Here, you'll find yourself seated atop meticulously polished horses, unicorns, and even the occasional dragon, all galloping in a circle of never-ending comparison. It's a ride that spins us round and round, through a whirlwind of vacations we can't afford, parties we weren't invited to, and milestones we haven't reached.

At first glance, the Carousel is a marvel to behold – a kaleidoscope of vibrant lives, each snapshot a testament to success, happiness, and perfection. But as the ride picks up speed, the colors blur, the music distorts, and the once joyful faces around us morph into masks of silent competition.

We begin by watching a friend's workout routine, feeling a twinge of admiration mixed with a dash of self-reproach. We witness another's home renovation, their shiny new kitchen tiles reflecting our own unspoken dissatisfaction. Then there's the colleague who, seemingly overnight, has become an overnight sensation, their every post garnished with a harvest of likes and comments, while our own notifications panel gathers dust.

This is the essence of the Comparison Carousel – the endless juxtaposition of our behind-the-scenes to everyone else's highlight reel. It spins a narrative of inadequacy, whispering that our lives, our achievements, our very selves are lacking. The Carousel is a cunning illusionist, convincing us that everyone else is living in a dream, while we're stuck in the waiting room of life.

But what toll does this constant comparison take on our mental health? It's like a slow drip of water on stone, gradually eroding our self-esteem. With each spin of the Carousel, our joy is chipped away, replaced by a gnawing hunger for validation and the fear of being left behind. It's a cycle that feeds anxiety, waters the seeds of depression, and plants insidious doubts about our paths.

Yet, hope is not lost. We can choose to step off the Carousel. We can learn to peer behind the curtain and see the sleight of hand for what it is. This chapter isn't just a tour of the dizzying ride; it's also a guide on how to slow it down, step back, and find contentment in our own journey, away from the constant glare of comparison.

We'll arm ourselves with the tools to dismantle the mechanisms of the Carousel: mindfulness to keep us grounded, gratitude to highlight the beauty in our lives, and the power of perspective to remind us that the only fair comparison is to who we were yesterday.

So, as the Carousel slows and the music fades, we find ourselves at a crossroads. Do we queue for another whirl, or do we take a breath, admire the craftsmanship of the ride, and choose to find joy in the stillness instead?

By the end of this chapter, you may just find yourself with a ticket in hand, deciding whether to ride again or to turn your back on the Carousel, walking towards a horizon painted with the hues of self-acceptance and genuine connection.

Chapter 2: The Privacy Illusion

Welcome to the grand theater of social media, where the stage is vast, and the audience is vast. Here, in the glow of our screens, we are all performers to some degree, sharing snippets of our lives with a sea of faces—some familiar, some strangers, and some, the unseen watchers in the wings.

In this chapter, we pull back the velvet curtains to reveal the illusion of privacy—a myth as pervasive as it is persistent. We begin with a simple truth: when it comes to social media, privacy is more of a suggestion than a guarantee. The moment we sign up and log in, we step into a space where the boundaries of personal space are as fluid as the terms and conditions we didn't read.

The allure of sharing is intoxicating. With each post, like, and share, we offer up pieces of ourselves, creating a mosaic that tells a story we hope is worth reading. Birthdays, anniversaries, the latte art in our morning coffee—all laid out for the world to see. But behind this open book, there's a network of silent scribes, taking notes on every chapter we unwittingly write.

The consequences of this over-sharing are often as invisible as they are insidious. We trade our data for convenience, our details for digital dopamine, and in the process, we craft a digital doppelgänger that knows more about us than we might care to admit. It knows our habits, our likes, our movements through the GPS pings we thought were private. It's a shadow that grows with every click, every check-in, and every photo tagged.

This isn't just about advertisers knowing which shoes you've been eyeing or the eerie precision of targeted ads. It's about the digital footprints that could lead to a breach of your personal security or affect your future job prospects. It's about the permanence of the internet, where a moment's indiscretion can become a lifetime's regret.

But fear not, for this chapter is not just a cautionary tale. It's also a treasure map, leading us to the vault where we can reclaim our privacy. We'll learn about the settings that tighten the curtains, the habits that keep our personal lives from becoming public domain, and the wisdom to discern what to share and what to safeguard.

We'll explore the art of selective sharing, the power of pausing before posting, and the liberation that comes from living in the moment, rather than for the 'gram. We'll consider how to curate our social media presence like a gallery, displaying only the pieces that speak to who we are without giving away the entire exhibition.

As we close the chapter on The Privacy Illusion, we'll be equipped not only with a better understanding of the mirage but with the tools to navigate the maze of social media with our privacy intact. We'll emerge wiser, more aware, and ready to engage with the digital world on our own terms, rather than playing the role of the unwitting spectator in the great performance of over-sharing.

Chapter 3: The Attention Economy

In the digital realm, where every swipe, tap, and click holds significance, attention is the ultimate currency. Social media platforms have mastered the art of capturing our focus, commodifying our time, and turning it into profit. In this chapter, we'll delve into the fascinating world of the attention economy, examining how your likes, shares, and time are the lifeblood of these platforms.

The Digital Gold Rush

Imagine for a moment that your attention is a finite resource. Every minute you spend scrolling through your social media feed is like a drop of gold in the vast river of content. Social media companies understand this concept all too well, and they have become experts at mining this digital gold.

Likes, shares, and comments are the modern-day nuggets of attention. They are the digital pats on the back that keep us engaged and craving more. When you receive a like on a post or a retweet of your clever remark, it triggers a small burst of dopamine in your brain, reinforcing the behavior. It's a subtle yet powerful reward system that keeps you scrolling, clicking, and interacting.

The Algorithmic Web

Behind the scenes, complex algorithms work tirelessly to ensure that you remain captivated. These algorithms are designed to analyze your behavior, preferences, and interactions to curate a personalized feed that maximizes your engagement. The more you engage, the more data you generate, and the more valuable you become to advertisers.

The attention economy extends beyond the platform itself. Advertisers are the ultimate beneficiaries, paying handsomely for access to your eyeballs. They bid for ad space based on your demographic information and online behavior. Your time spent on the platform and your interactions contribute to the platform's revenue. In essence, you are the product being sold to the highest bidder.

The Cost of Attention

While social media platforms may appear free at first glance, they exact a high price in the form of your attention. Hours slip away as you scroll through endless posts and videos. Productivity takes a hit, and real-life experiences often pale in comparison to the curated content on your screen.

Moreover, the quest for attention can have profound effects on mental health. The constant comparison to others, the pressure to craft the perfect post, and the fear of missing out (FOMO) are just a few of the emotional tolls exacted by the attention economy. The dopamine-driven feedback loop can lead to addictive behaviors, making it challenging to break free from the digital grasp.

Taking Control

Understanding the attention economy is the first step toward regaining control over your time and focus. Recognize that your attention is a valuable resource, and consider how you allocate it. Are you spending it on meaningful connections, personal growth, and real-life experiences? Or is it slipping through your fingers as you mindlessly scroll through an endless sea of content?

In the next chapter, we will explore the echo chamber effect, where algorithms can limit your exposure to diverse perspectives and trap you in a loop of similar opinions. But before we venture further into the digital labyrinth, take a moment to reflect on your own interactions with the attention economy. Are you a conscious consumer of content, or are you unwittingly caught in its grip?

Chapter 4: The Echo Chamber Effect

In the vast digital landscape of social media, it's easy to believe that we're exposed to a multitude of perspectives and opinions. However, beneath the surface, a subtle force is at play—the echo chamber effect. In this chapter, we'll explore how algorithms shape our online experience, often leading us to encounter ideas and views that align with our existing beliefs while isolating us from differing viewpoints.

The Algorithmic Filter Bubble

Imagine social media platforms as digital curators, tailoring the content you see to match your preferences. This personalization is made possible by algorithms that analyze your past behavior, likes, shares, and comments to determine what content is most likely to engage you. While this can enhance your user experience, it comes at a cost—the creation of filter bubbles.

Filter bubbles are self-reinforcing information ecosystems that prioritize content you're likely to agree with. If you're passionate about a particular political ideology, for instance, the algorithm will present you with posts and articles that confirm your beliefs. Over time, this curated content shapes your perspective and can lead to the illusion that everyone shares your views.

The Polarization Predicament

One of the most concerning consequences of the echo chamber effect is the polarization of society. When individuals are exposed only to information and opinions that validate their existing beliefs, it becomes increasingly challenging to empathize with differing viewpoints. This polarization can foster hostility and deepen divisions in society, as people retreat to their ideological safe spaces.

The echo chamber effect isn't solely about politics. It applies to various aspects of our lives, from lifestyle choices to hobbies. Consider how your social media feed might reinforce your interests and hobbies, steering you away from exploring new experiences or perspectives.

Breaking the Echo Chamber

Breaking free from the echo chamber requires conscious effort. It involves actively seeking out diverse sources of information and engaging in respectful discussions with individuals who hold differing opinions. It means acknowledging that your feed may not always align with the broader reality.

Social media platforms, too, have a role to play in addressing this issue. They can implement features that encourage users to explore diverse content and engage with perspectives outside their filter bubbles. But ultimately, it's up to each user to take control of their digital experience.

The Power of Critical Thinking

In a world where algorithms curate our information diet, critical thinking becomes more critical than ever. It's essential to approach online content with a discerning eye, questioning the sources and biases behind the information. Encouraging open dialogue and respectful debate can help bridge the gap between echo chambers and foster a more nuanced and interconnected online community.

As we navigate the digital landscape, remember that diversity of thought enriches our understanding of the world. In the next chapter, we'll explore how the incessant pull of social media can consume our precious time. But before we delve into that, take a moment to reflect on your own digital echo chamber. Are you exposed to a wide range of perspectives, or are you inadvertently trapped in a loop of similar opinions?

Chapter 5: The Time Vampire

Tick, tock, scroll, repeat. The endless vortex of social media has a voracious appetite for your time, and it's often hard to escape its clutches. In this chapter, we'll take a lighthearted yet sobering look at how social media transforms into a time vampire, draining away precious hours that could be spent on more meaningful pursuits.

The Infinite Scroll

We've all been there—just a quick check of your social media feed before starting your day, and suddenly, hours have vanished like a puff of smoke. The infinite scroll feature, designed to keep you engaged, can feel like an inescapable time warp. You start with good intentions, but the gravitational pull of never-ending content keeps you trapped.

The Illusion of Productivity

Social media platforms have a sneaky way of making you feel productive. You might convince yourself that you're keeping up with the latest news or staying connected with friends and family. However, when you look back at those hours spent scrolling, what tangible accomplishments do you have to show for them?

The Opportunity Cost

Every moment spent on social media comes with an opportunity cost. While you're engrossed in the virtual world, real-life opportunities slip through your fingers. The book you wanted to read, the hobby you wanted to pursue, the exercise routine you planned—all fall victim to the time vampire's insatiable appetite.

The Humorous Side

Let's not forget the humorous aspects of this time-consuming habit. Memes, funny videos, and relatable posts have a way of tickling our funny bones. Social media can be a source of entertainment and laughter. However, it's important to strike a balance and ensure that humor doesn't overshadow the more serious consequences of excessive screen time.

Reclaiming Your Time

Breaking free from the clutches of the time vampire requires a conscious effort. Consider implementing time management techniques, such as setting limits on your social media usage or scheduling dedicated "digital detox" hours. Take inventory of how you spend your time and ask yourself: What could I accomplish if I reclaimed those lost hours?

Rediscovering the Present

The real world is a treasure trove of experiences waiting to be uncovered. Whether it's exploring new hobbies, spending quality time with loved ones, or pursuing personal goals, the possibilities are endless. Social media can be a valuable tool, but it should never overshadow the richness of life outside the screen.

As we move forward in this exploration of the impact of social media, keep in mind that time is a finite and precious resource. In the next chapter, we'll examine how the stress of the digital age can amplify when combined with social media. But before we delve into that, take a moment to reflect on your own relationship with the time vampire. Are there changes you'd like to make to regain control of your time?

Chapter 6: The Stress Amplifier

In the age of digital connectivity, social media has become both a lifeline and a source of stress for many. In this chapter, we'll dive into the complex relationship between social media use and elevated stress levels, exploring the factors that contribute to this modern-day dilemma.

The FOMO Phenomenon

Fear of Missing Out (FOMO) is a powerful force that lurks in the background of our online experiences. As we scroll through the carefully curated highlights of others' lives, it's easy to feel left out or inadequate. The constant comparison to idealized versions of reality can lead to feelings of anxiety and stress.

The Pressure to Perform

In the world of social media, appearances matter. The pressure to maintain a polished online persona can be overwhelming. Posting the perfect picture, crafting witty captions, and garnering likes and comments can become a source of immense stress. The quest for validation in the form of virtual applause can take a toll on mental well-being.

Information Overload

The digital age bombards us with a constant stream of information, much of it negative or anxiety-inducing. News articles, status updates, and viral content often focus on crises, conflicts, and controversies. The unrelenting exposure to distressing news can contribute to heightened stress levels, leaving us feeling overwhelmed and helpless.

Social Comparison and Envy

Social media invites us to peer into the lives of others, and it's easy to fixate on what we lack in comparison. Envy, jealousy, and feelings of inadequacy can fester as we scroll through feeds filled with seemingly perfect lives. These emotions, when left unchecked, can contribute to chronic stress and even impact our self-esteem.

The 24/7 Connection

The boundary between work and personal life has become increasingly blurred in the digital age. Constant connectivity means that notifications and work-related messages can intrude into our personal time, creating a sense of always being "on call." This constant pressure to be available can lead to chronic stress and burnout.

Coping Strategies

Recognizing the link between social media use and stress is the first step toward managing this digital-induced anxiety. Implementing healthy boundaries, such as designated screen-free times and spaces, can provide relief. Additionally, mindfulness techniques, such as meditation and deep breathing, can help mitigate the impact of social media stress.

Finding Balance

Social media is not inherently evil, but its unchecked use can contribute to elevated stress levels. Striking a balance between the digital world and the real world is key to managing stress effectively. Remember that your well-being is paramount, and taking proactive steps to reduce the stressors associated with social media is a worthwhile endeavor.

As we continue our journey through the complex landscape of social media's impact on our lives, keep in mind the toll it can take on your mental health. In the next chapter, we'll explore the pursuit of authenticity in an age of carefully curated feeds. But before we delve into that, take a moment to reflect on your own experiences with social media-related stress. Are there changes you'd like to make to find a healthier balance?

Chapter 7: The Authenticity Mirage

In the age of social media, authenticity has become a highly prized virtue. We're encouraged to share our unfiltered selves, to embrace vulnerability, and to be genuine in our interactions. But is this quest for authenticity on social media all it appears to be? In this chapter, we'll explore the complexities of authenticity in a world of carefully curated feeds.

The Perfectly Imperfect Facade

Scroll through your social media feed, and you'll encounter a world of picturesque moments and polished appearances. It's a realm where everyone seems to have it all together, showcasing the highlights of their lives. However, beneath these carefully curated images lies a paradox— the quest for authenticity often results in the creation of an inauthentic facade.

The Pressure to Perform Authenticity

Ironically, the pursuit of authenticity can become another performance. There's pressure to share personal struggles, to expose vulnerabilities, and to be transparent about one's life. While these efforts can be genuine, they can also be performative, driven by a desire for likes, shares, and validation.

The Filtered Reality

Filters, photo editing, and the art of cropping have become commonplace on social media. These tools allow users to present themselves and their experiences in the best possible light. While there's nothing inherently wrong with enhancing photos, it can blur the line between authenticity and artifice.

The Fear of Judgment

The fear of judgment from peers and followers can deter individuals from sharing their true selves. It's easy to self-censor and conform to social norms to avoid potential criticism. In this way, the pursuit of authenticity can be stifled by the pressure to conform to the expectations of the digital crowd.

The Quest for Connection

Authenticity remains a noble goal in the digital realm. It fosters genuine connections and humanizes our online interactions. The challenge lies in striking a balance between sharing authentically and avoiding the pitfalls of performative authenticity.

Finding True Authenticity

True authenticity doesn't always manifest in the form of personal confessions or displays of vulnerability. It can also be found in genuine interactions, supportive communities, and honest conversations. Authenticity is about being true to oneself while respecting the boundaries and comfort levels of others.

Embracing Complexity

The journey toward authenticity on social media is a complex one. It's not about conforming to an idealized notion of vulnerability but rather about embracing the multidimensional nature of humanity. Authenticity allows for the full range of human experiences, including joy, sorrow, success, and struggle.

As we navigate the terrain of social media, remember that authenticity is a personal and evolving journey. In the next chapter, we'll explore how the late-night scrolling habit can impact our sleep and well-being. But before we delve into that, take a moment to reflect on your own experiences with authenticity on social media. How do you balance the desire to be authentic with the pressures of digital performance?

Chapter 8: The Sleep Thief

As the day winds down and darkness falls, many of us seek refuge in the comforting glow of our screens. Whether it's catching up on social media feeds, watching videos, or engaging in late-night chats, our devices have become companions in the nighttime hours. But in this chapter, we'll explore the hidden cost of late-night scrolling—the theft of our precious sleep.

The Blue-Light Dilemma

The screens we hold in our hands emit a type of light known as blue light. This artificial light can disrupt our natural sleep-wake cycle by suppressing the production of melatonin, the hormone responsible for regulating sleep. When we expose ourselves to screens late at night, we're essentially telling our bodies to stay awake.

The Rabbit Hole Effect

Late-night scrolling often leads to the "rabbit hole" phenomenon, where a quick check of social media turns into an hours-long expedition. Time seems to fly by as we navigate from post to post, video to video. The relentless stream of content entices us, making it difficult to tear ourselves away and head to bed.

Sleep Deprivation's Toll

Consistently sacrificing sleep for screen time takes a toll on our health and well-being. Sleep deprivation can lead to a range of issues, including impaired cognitive function, reduced focus, increased stress, and even physical health problems. It's a silent thief that slowly erodes our vitality.

The Disruption of Sleep Hygiene

Our devices disrupt not only our sleep patterns but also our sleep hygiene. The habits we establish before bedtime significantly impact the quality of our sleep. Late-night scrolling can replace calming pre-sleep routines with stimulating content, making it harder for our minds to wind down.

Breaking the Habit

Breaking the habit of late-night scrolling requires intention and discipline. Implementing a digital curfew, where screens are put away an hour or so before bedtime, can be a game-changer. Engaging in relaxing activities like reading, meditation, or gentle stretching can help signal to your body that it's time to rest.

Reclaiming Your Sleep

Prioritizing sleep is an act of self-care. It's about recognizing the value of rest and restoration in our lives. As you embark on a journey to reclaim your sleep, remember that the benefits extend far beyond the nighttime hours. Improved sleep leads to greater productivity, better mood, and enhanced overall well-being.

The Balance of Connection and Rest

While our devices can connect us to the world, it's crucial to strike a balance between staying connected and prioritizing rest. The allure of late-night scrolling may be strong, but the rewards of a good night's sleep are immeasurable.

In the next chapter, we'll explore how social media can impact our real-life relationships and communication. But before we delve into that, take a moment to reflect on your own experiences with late-night scrolling. Are there changes you'd like to make to ensure a more restful night's sleep?

Chapter 9: The Relationship Saboteur

In the interconnected world of social media, our relationships and communication have undergone a transformation. While these platforms promise to bring us closer, they can also unwittingly drive a wedge between us and the people we care about most. In this chapter, we'll explore how social media can become a relationship saboteur.

The Attention Divide

In the digital age, our attention is a finite resource, and social media competes for a significant share of it. When we prioritize screen time over face-to-face interactions, we risk neglecting the people we love. Partners, family members, and friends may feel sidelined or unimportant when our screens take precedence.

The Illusion of Connection

Social media can create the illusion of connection without the depth of genuine interaction. Liking a post or sending a quick message can give the impression of staying connected, but it often falls short of meaningful conversation. These superficial interactions can erode the quality of our real-life relationships.

The Comparisons and Envy

Scrolling through the highlight reels of others' lives can lead to a phenomenon known as "comparison envy." We compare our own lives to the seemingly perfect lives of our peers, which can foster feelings of inadequacy and discontent. This negative mindset can spill over into our real-life relationships, leading to resentment or strained interactions.

The Digital Conflicts

Misunderstandings and conflicts can easily arise in the realm of social media. What might have been a simple disagreement in person can escalate into a heated online argument, often with an audience. These digital conflicts can strain real-life relationships, causing emotional rifts that are challenging to mend.

The Invasion of Privacy

Sharing personal moments and information on social media can inadvertently breach the privacy of our loved ones. Posting without their consent or sharing intimate details of our relationships can create discomfort and mistrust. The line between public and private becomes blurred, and boundaries are crossed.

Fostering Real-Life Connections

While social media offers opportunities for connection, it's essential to balance digital interactions with real-life ones. Prioritizing in-person conversations, quality time, and active listening can strengthen our relationships. It's also crucial to be mindful of the impact our online behavior can have on those we care about.

Open Communication

Healthy relationships thrive on open and honest communication. Addressing concerns, setting boundaries, and discussing the role of social media in your relationship can lead to a deeper understanding and a more harmonious balance between the digital and real worlds.

Reconnecting with Presence

Reconnecting with presence means being fully engaged in the moment, whether you're spending time with loved ones or enjoying personal experiences. Put down your devices, look up from your screens, and cherish the connections that matter most in your life.

As we continue our exploration of the impact of social media on our lives, remember that real-life relationships are the foundation of our happiness and well-being. In the next chapter, we'll reflect on the overall cost of social media in our lives and whether it's worth it. But before we delve into that, take a moment to consider your own experiences with the potential impact of social media on your relationships. Are there changes you'd like to make to nurture these connections?

Chapter 10: The Final Straw: Is It Worth It?

As we conclude our journey through the complex landscape of social media, it's time to take a step back and reflect. We've explored the various facets of this digital world, from the allure of connection to the hidden costs of late-night scrolling. Now, we turn our attention to the ultimate question: Is it worth it?

The Personal Stories

Throughout this book, we've woven personal stories of individuals who have grappled with the impact of social media on their lives. These stories have showcased the struggles, the victories, and the transformative moments that social media can bring. They've underscored the complexity of this digital landscape and the diverse ways in which it affects us.

The Research Insights

In addition to personal narratives, we've delved into the world of research to better understand the effects of social media. Studies have explored topics such as mental health, attention span, sleep quality, and the impact on relationships. The findings paint a nuanced picture of the digital age, highlighting both the benefits and the drawbacks of social media.

Weighing the Costs

As we reflect on the journey, it's crucial to weigh the costs and benefits of social media in our lives. The true cost encompasses not only the time spent scrolling but also the impact on our mental health, relationships, and overall well-being. It's a multifaceted evaluation that requires honest introspection.

The Value of Connection

For many, social media provides a valuable avenue for connection. It bridges geographical distances, fosters communities, and enables communication with loved ones. It can be a source of inspiration, support, and empowerment.

The Price of Distraction

On the flip side, social media's constant allure can steal our focus, hinder our productivity, and perpetuate the culture of distraction. It's easy to become ensnared in the digital world at the expense of our real-life experiences and goals.

The Pursuit of Balance

Ultimately, the decision to engage with social media is a personal one. It involves finding a balance that aligns with your values, priorities, and well-being. It means being intentional about your digital interactions and recognizing when it's time to disconnect.

The Power of Choice

Social media is a tool, and like any tool, its impact depends on how it's used. By acknowledging the potential costs and benefits, you empower yourself to make informed choices. You can choose to engage with social media mindfully, with an awareness of its influence on your life.

A Digital Detox

If you find that social media has encroached upon your well-being, consider embarking on a digital detox. It's a chance to disconnect, recalibrate, and rediscover the richness of life outside the screen.

The Unwritten Chapters

Our exploration of social media is far from over. The digital landscape continues to evolve, and new chapters are being written every day. As you navigate this ever-changing terrain, remember that you hold the pen to your own story, and you have the power to shape your digital narrative.

The Final Reflection

As we close this chapter and the book as a whole, take a moment to reflect on your own relationship with social media. Consider the costs and benefits it brings into your life. Is it worth it? The answer, like social media itself, is deeply personal.

Conclusion: Life After the 'Log Out' Button

In the preceding chapters, we've embarked on a journey through the complex world of social media. We've explored its myriad facets, from the allure of connection to the hidden costs it can exact on our time, mental health, and relationships. As we conclude this book, let's envision a life beyond the 'log out' button—a life that balances our digital and real-world experiences.

Rediscovering the Real World

It's easy to forget that not too long ago, our ancestors lived rich, full lives without the digital distractions of social media. They connected with one another through face-to-face interactions, shared stories around campfires, and cultivated relationships within their communities. In many ways, their lives were a testament to the depth and richness of human connection.

Embracing the Balance

While social media has undeniably reshaped the way we connect and communicate, it's essential to strike a balance between the digital and analog worlds. The 'log out' button becomes a tool for regaining control over our time, attention, and well-being.

Tips for a Digital Detox

If you find that social media has become a consuming force in your life, consider embarking on a digital detox. Here are some tips to help you get started:

1. **Set Boundaries:** Establish specific times and spaces where screens are off-limits. Create designated 'no-phone zones' in your home and carve out screen-free hours in your day.

2. **Mindful Consumption:** Be conscious of the content you consume. Follow accounts and communities that inspire and uplift you. Unfollow or mute content that brings negativity or stress into your life.

3. **Digital Curfew:** Implement a digital curfew, where screens are put away at least an hour before bedtime. This allows your brain to wind down and prepares you for a restful night's sleep.

4. **Regular Disconnect:** Consider taking regular breaks from social media, whether it's for a day, a weekend, or longer periods. Use this time to reconnect with hobbies, nature, and loved ones.

5. **Quality Over Quantity:** Prioritize quality interactions over quantity. Engage in meaningful conversations, both online and offline. Foster genuine connections that enrich your life.

6. **Practice Gratitude:** Cultivate gratitude for the real-world experiences and relationships that bring joy and fulfillment to your life. Keep a gratitude journal to remind yourself of the blessings beyond the screen.

A Future of Choice

As we look toward the future, remember that social media is a tool—one that you have the power to shape and control. The decisions you make about your digital interactions are deeply personal and reflect your values, priorities, and well-being. Choose wisely, and always be mindful of the impact these choices have on your life.

The Unwritten Chapters

The journey through the digital landscape continues to unfold, with new technologies, platforms, and challenges emerging. As you navigate this ever-evolving terrain, take the lessons learned from this exploration with you. Keep the 'log out' button close at hand, ready to reclaim your time and rediscover the world beyond the screen.

Appendix A: Social Media Detox Challenge

Welcome to the Social Media Detox Challenge! In the next 30 days, you'll embark on a journey to rekindle your connection with the real world, reduce your digital dependence, and regain control over your time and attention. Each day, you'll find a new activity designed to help you break free from the digital realm and rediscover the richness of life outside the screen.

Day 1: Unfollow Negative Accounts

Start by unfollowing accounts that bring negativity or stress into your social media feed. Surround yourself with content that inspires and uplifts you.

Day 2: Set a Digital Curfew

Designate a specific time in the evening to put away your devices. Use this time for relaxation, reading, or quality time with loved ones.

Day 3: Practice Mindful Scrolling

Today, practice mindful scrolling. Pay attention to the content you consume and how it makes you feel. Unfollow accounts that no longer align with your interests or values.

Day 4: Go for a Screen-Free Walk

Take a walk without your phone. Focus on the sights, sounds, and sensations of the real world around you.

Day 5: Phone-Free Meals

Enjoy your meals without the distraction of your phone. Savor the flavors and engage in meaningful conversation with those you dine with.

Day 6: Rediscover a Hobby

Revisit a hobby or activity you used to enjoy before social media became a significant part of your life. Dedicate time to it today.

Day 7: Reach Out to a Friend

Send a heartfelt message or make a phone call to a friend you haven't connected with in a while. Nurture real-world relationships.

Day 8: Create a Digital-Free Zone

Designate a room or space in your home as a digital-free zone. Use it for reading, relaxation, or quality time with family.

Day 9: Mindful Morning Routine

Start your day mindfully. Avoid checking your phone first thing in the morning. Instead, engage in a calming morning routine.

Day 10: Write a Letter

Write a handwritten letter to a loved one. Express your thoughts and feelings on paper. It's a meaningful way to connect.

Day 11: Practice Gratitude

Start a gratitude journal. Write down three things you're grateful for every day. Focus on the positive aspects of your life.

Day 12: Explore Nature

Spend time in nature today. Whether it's a hike, a picnic, or simply sitting in a park, reconnect with the natural world.

Day 13: Organize a Digital Declutter

Clean up your digital life. Delete unused apps, organize your files, and declutter your email inbox.

Day 14: Volunteer or Help Others

Engage in an act of kindness or volunteer your time to help others in your community. Real-world connections are built on compassion.

Day 15: Digital Detox Day

Take a full day away from social media and digital devices. Use this time to reflect, relax, and engage in offline activities.

Day 16: Explore Local Culture

Visit a local museum, art gallery, or cultural event. Immerse yourself in the culture of your community.

Day 17: Practice Mindfulness

Begin a mindfulness meditation practice. It helps you stay present and reduce digital distractions.

Day 18: Host a Device-Free Dinner

Invite friends or family over for a device-free dinner. Enjoy each other's company without screens.

Day 19: Take a New Route

Change up your routine by taking a different route to work or exploring a new neighborhood in your city.

Day 20: Learn Something New

Start learning a new skill or taking up a new hobby you've always wanted to try.

Day 21: Capture Memories

Take photos or journal about your offline experiences. Create tangible memories of your journey.

Day 22: Digital Art Detox

Try your hand at creating art without digital tools. Draw, paint, or craft something by hand.

Day 23: Reconnect with a Childhood Friend

Reach out to an old friend from your childhood. Rekindle connections from the past.

Day 24: Attend a Live Event

Go to a live event, such as a concert, play, or sports game. Immerse yourself in the real-world experience.

Day 25: Share Your Journey

Share your detox journey with others. Encourage friends or family to join you on the path to a healthier digital life.

Day 26: Disconnect from Social Media Apps

Temporarily remove social media apps from your phone to reduce temptation.

Day 27: Reflect on Your Progress

Take some time to reflect on the changes you've noticed in your life since starting the challenge.

Day 28: Plan Digital-Free Days

Schedule regular digital detox days into your calendar for the future.

Day 29: Connect with Nature

Spend a day in nature, whether it's a hike, a day at the beach, or simply enjoying a local park.

Day 30: Celebrate Your Achievements

Celebrate completing the 30-day Social Media Detox Challenge. Reflect on the positive impact it has had on your life and consider how you'll continue to maintain a healthy balance between the digital and real worlds.

Appendix B: A Modest Poem About Why Thou Shouldst Delete Thy Social Media

*Please consider reading section this out loud to a close friend.

*Oh, weary souls in this digital age, I entreat thee, lend me thine ears,
For in verses akin to tales of old, I beseech thee, quell thy fears.*

*Of reasons why, mayhaps, thou shouldst partake, In severing thy
bond with social media's wake.*

*In the realm of cyberspace, we doth abide, where ceaseless scrolls
do unfold, Yet in pursuit of endless likes, we barter life's true gold.*

*The friendships once so tender, now avatars at hand, Hold greater
worth in flesh and blood, upon real-world's tranquil strand.*

*Comparison's cruel masquerade, in social media's grand charade,
Leaves naught but shattered mirrors, where self-esteem does fade.*

*Why gauge thine worth in hearts or thumbs, in likes and comments
won? When life's true value lies in joy, beneath each waking sun.*

*Filters and edits, they craft a false facade, We chase perfection in
the pixels, forsaking the real and flawed.*

*Yet life's true beauty doth reside in flaws, and moments unrefined, In
laughter shared with kindred souls, in hearts and spirits intertwined.*

*The ceaseless stream of news, it fills our burdened minds, With tales
of sorrow and anger, in a world that often blinds.*

*Unplug from this torrent, seek solace, and breathe anew, For
happiness is found in peace, and moments not bathed in blue.*

*The screens that steal our slumber, with late-night scrolling's throes,
Replace our dreams with vacant posts, as restful slumber goes.*

Embrace the tranquil darkness, let sleep rekindle grace, For in its gentle cradle, dream's wonders shall we chase.

The hours we yield to pixels, they pilfer our precious time, From human touch and laughter, from nature's scenes sublime.

Trade screen's embrace for adventure's quest, for memories to unfurl, In the arms of nature's beauty, where wonders and joys swirl.

Oh, gentle souls, ponder this, a humble and heartfelt plea, Look beyond the glowing screens, set thy spirit truly free.

Life's beauty lies in moments, in each laugh and tear, So tread the path with open eyes, in a world unburdened, clear.

Delete, deactivate, log out, and rediscover life's grace, In every smile, in every mile, in the world's wide embrace.

Embrace simplicity's pleasures, in true connections, see, For life is genuinely splendid, without the chains of social media, be free.

Forever, and ever—

And ever.

www.ingramcontent.com/pod-product-compliance
Lightning Source LLC
LaVergne TN
LVHW051633050326
832903LV00033B/4734